Joseph's Coat of Many Colours

Joseph was the youngest of many brothers.
His father loved him very much.

Joseph's father had a coat made for him,
woven of bright colours.

Joseph's brothers were jealous. They said,
"Our father never gave us bright coats."

One day, the brothers were out with
their sheep when Joseph came to see them.

They took Joseph's bright coat away
and sold him as a slave.

They put goat's blood on Joseph's coat
and showed it to their father.

He cried aloud, saying, "My son Joseph has been eaten by a wild animal."

Joseph was taken to work in faraway Egypt.

But God loved him and took care of him.
Joseph became more and more powerful.

Finally, he worked for the mighty king
of Egypt, the pharaoh.
Joseph was like a prince now.

He wore a gold chain and rode in a chariot
but he missed his family.

Joseph heard there was a famine in his home land.
People were starving without food.

One day, travellers came to buy corn
from Joseph. He was amazed to see them;
they were his brothers!

Joseph asked, "Is my father alive?"
and his brothers said yes. Joseph said,
"Here in Egypt, God has blessed me.

Go and bring my father, and your families, and your animals, here to Egypt."

Joseph was very happy when his
family arrived. He took care of everyone
and gave them food and new homes.